Forex
A Newbies' Guide

An Everyday Guide to
Foreign Currency Trading

Alan Northcott

www.alannorthcott.com

www.newbiesguidetoforex.com

Copyright Notice

Table of Contents

Introduction

Many people are drawn to the prospect of Forex trading because they have heard about the leverage that can be employed, using a small amount of money to control a large amount of money, and therefore with the possibility of making money much faster than you could by simply investing in, say, stocks.

These people have also, probably, read the warnings in other books and courses, the ones that point out that leverage or gearing of your money is a double-edged sword, and can result in losses much greater than your initial stake – but they may try to ignore it.

If you think about it, it is obvious that more is lost by Forex traders than gained. Simply, every trade has two sides, or two parties to the transaction, each of whom thinks they are going to gain. What one wins, the other loses. And although you do not pay direct commissions for Forex transactions, there is a difference between the buying and selling prices, called the spread, which effectively takes a little out of each deal for the Forex broker. Therefore, traders as a whole finish worse off.

The statistics are actually a little worse than that would imply. It's estimated that more than 80% (some say 90%) of would-be traders fail and have to give up. You see the ones that succeed are continually taking beginners to the cleaners. They need a constant fresh supply of novice traders and their funds, so they can continue to enjoy their success.

So does that mean you should give up now and save your money? The answer for some people is probably. If you're going to compete with the experts, then you cannot expect to do so simply by buying a $97 "Forex robot", or by looking for a secret trick that you can implement in 5 minutes. You need to be prepared to study and analyze the markets, and to make sensible decisions, and even then no one with realistic knowledge of the markets is going to guarantee that you will make a profit. If you want to take on the challenge, pitting your wits and knowledge against others, then read on to gain an understanding of the task at hand.

"Life is a journey, not a destination" – Ralph Waldo Emerson. So it is with trading. You do not "learn trading" and then go off for 30 years making money on the markets. You need to stay fresh and open to current ideas by continuing your trading education. Though the basics of trading are (relatively) immutable, you should consider this book simply the start of your trading education and career. It is the author's intent to give you the best grounding possible, so that you can look forward to a long and successful vocation.

I have set up a companion website especially for this book, called www.newbiesguidetoforex.com. I hope you will visit it and look around, as I have reproduced all the diagrams there (for clarity) and have set up a forum for discussions – with your help, we will get an active Forex group going!

A.N.

P.S. I am excited to report that I recently acquired the rights to sell a comprehensive Forex video course, composed by another trader, and have a special discount for readers of this book. This goes into much greater depth, for those who want to take the topic to the next level.

Simply go to the companion website www.newbiesguidetoforex.com/membersarea for full details of the offer.

Forex Essentials

Forex, or foreign exchange, is simply the buying of one currency with another currency, with the hope that your transactions will be profitable. It is only in recent years that it has become so popular, because the Internet and changes in regulations have allowed individual traders to have access to the markets and potentially do well.

Without making this a history lesson, just as background you should know that currencies used to be tied to the "gold standard", which means you could in theory going to the bank and ask for the equivalent value of gold for your currency. Those days disappeared, particularly as more currency had to be printed to cope with the costs of world war, and there just wasn't enough gold to back it up. The US dollar took over from the British pound as the reserve currency, and everything was more or less pegged to the dollar.

But with various and diverse economies, it was difficult to keep currencies pegged to each other, so in 1978 the International Monetary Fund allowed currencies to float and find their own values relative to others. (A similar thing is happening now with the euro, where diverse economies are finding it increasingly hard to maintain a fixed currency relationship – "those who do not learn from history are doomed forever to repeat it").

In the United States currency trading was still reserved for the large financial houses and banks, but the law changed in 2000 to allow individual traders access. One of the attractions of the Forex market is that, unlike stock markets and particularly "small cap stocks", the market is relatively open and unlikely to be manipulated. There is no central market such as a stock market, as each country has its own dealings, with all of them interconnected electronically.

It is estimated that about $4 trillion is traded every day, meaning that even the largest banks cannot unduly affect the prices. Add to this the fact that there is a 24-hour market, 5 1/2 days a week, and regardless of when you go to work you can always find time to do some Forex trading. And you can always trade, unlike stocks, as there are plenty of market participants. This is called liquidity.

There are no fees, as such. There is a microscopic difference between the prices you can "buy" and "sell" at, as you will see, and because of the enormous size of currency "lots" that you deal in, this microscopic difference mounts up and pays for the broker's services.

The Basic Concepts

Firstly, currencies are always traded and quoted in pairs, for example the US dollar and the pound sterling, or the Swiss franc and the Japanese yen. You "buy" one currency, simultaneously "selling" the other. And you get to choose which one you buy and which you sell, it's not like a share transaction where you are already holding some stocks, and so have to sell those.

I put buy and selling in quotes above, as you really don't need to have the cash to do either. Those are the transactions that you commit to, but as you'll find out you do not need to, for instance, have a bank account full of Swiss francs in order to sell them.

Forex trading is based on a standard lot size of $100,000, or 100,000 currency units if something other than the US dollar is first in the pairing. You can also trade mini lots, which are 10% of that size, $10,000, and even smaller micro-lots if you want to start cheaply. How much money you will need to open the trade depends on your broker, who among other things will assess your credit worthiness, simply to make sure that if you make a losing trade, you will be able to cover the loss. Typically you may get a ratio of 100 to 1, which would mean you need $1000 to trade a standard lot of $100,000.

When you go to enter a trade, you will see the currency pair, for example USDCAD which means US dollar and Canadian dollar, and two numbers, for example 1.0242 and 1.0245, called the "bid" and the "ask", or the "sell" and "buy". The first currency mentioned, in this case the US dollar, is the base currency, and the number given represents the amount of the second currency, or "counter currency" needed to buy one unit of the base currency. In other words, one US dollar equals 1.024X Canadian dollars.

The bid price or sell price is how much of the counter currency you get for each unit of the base currency, in other words if you were buying Canadian dollars using US dollars – you are "selling" US dollars; the ask price is how much of the second currency you need to buy a unit of the base currency, in other words how many Canadian dollars you need to buy one US dollar. The difference between the numbers is called the spread, and that is how much the broker gets to keep for doing the transaction.

In case 3/100ths of a cent (in this case) doesn't sound like much, you shouldn't worry for the broker. Remember you are dealing in units of $100,000, so the actual amount of spread for one standard lot is $30, in this case.

The Symbols

Unlike stocks, you only have a few main symbols to remember.

USD – US dollar

EUR – Euro

GBP – British pound sterling

CAD – Canadian dollar

AUD – Australian dollar

CHF – Swiss franc

JPY – Japanese yen

There are dozens of other currencies, such as the Mexican peso, Thailand baht, etc., but the ones above are the ones that most Forex traders use all the time. The six major currency pairs that are traded the most are EURUSD, USDJPY, GBPUSD, USDCHF, USDCHD, and USDAUD.

The Pip

You won't go far in the Forex field before you encounter the "pip". This stands for "percentage in point", which means a percent of a percent, the same as the fourth decimal place. So in the example above of the

USDCAD, it is the last number quoted (except you must watch out, as some brokers quote you five decimal places).

As the quote was 1.0242 – 1.0245, you can see that the spread between the bid and the ask was three pips in this case. Suppose the price changes to 1.0295 – 1.0298. That means it has risen 0.0053, or 53 pips. For a standard lot, this would work out to $530 profit or loss (more or less, as the spread between the bid and ask would also have to accounted for, depending whether you bought or sold).

The Margin

With any sort of financial trading, if you do not have to put up all the money in advance you are "trading on margin". This applies to Forex, commodities or futures, and any similar scheme.

Trading on margin is a great thing if you are winning, and trading on margin can be disastrous if you're losing. It just multiplies the effect of the money you have. It is like your broker is making you a loan for the amount you commit to, and as it is only a loan if you lose you must pay it back.

What this means is that you can "lose more than the money in your account". In fact you don't, because you have to keep filling up your account, drawing money from other resources whenever your broker says you're running short, which is called a "margin call".

If you only ever made winning trades, then you would never risk a margin call. If you trade well within the amount of money that you have in your account, then you may avoid a margin call. But if you do get a margin call because an active trade has slipped too far against you, you have to answer it very quickly by putting money in your brokerage account. There is no time to sell some equity; you need to have the cash available.

If you do not respond immediately to a margin call, then the broker is allowed to knock you out of any or all of your trades to protect his position. He doesn't have to pay any attention to which trades you wanted to hang on to, he can just go blindly closing them all at what may be inopportune times to minimize his exposure.

Even then, he is still entitled to the money you have lost, if he is not able to get it from your account and from closing your trades. It can get very nasty.

Trading on margin is an inherent part of the system, and the reason that you have the opportunity for good profits on Forex. You must realize that you should treat the margin with respect, before it demands your attention.

The Mechanics

So that's the principle, but is probably best to go through that example exactly, just so you can see how it works out. For simplicity, I'll show you an example with the US dollar as the counter currency, as it is easy to work out the value of each pip. By the way, it doesn't matter what currency your account is in, you can trade in any of the currency pairs and your broker will figure out how much you won or lost.

So for this example, look at the EURUSD. The current quote is 1.36994 – 1.37016. Assume you "buy" one standard lot of Euros, which is €100,000. This would be at the ask price of 1.37016.

Say the price of the EURUSD goes up, the same as the euro going up in value or the dollar going down, relatively. Making the maths easy, maybe the quote goes up by 50 pips, to 1.37494 – 1.37516 (remembering that the pip is the fourth decimal place, and these prices show five decimal places).

If you close your trade, it will be at the bid price of 1.37494. Therefore you have gained 1.37494 minus 1.37016, or 0.00478 – 47.8 pips. It is not 50 because of the spread, the broker's cut.

When the US dollar is the counter currency, every pip you gain is worth $10 when trading a standard lot. Therefore you have made $478 on the trade.

To be able to make this trade, typically you would need €1000 or the equivalent in your account with the standard 1 to 100 leverage.

This example shows you the power of the leverage, which should excite you; but you must also realize that the power works the other way, and magnifies your losses. And whatever anyone tells you, no one can guarantee you're going to win on any particular trade, so it is your personal responsibility to make sure that you do not over leverage your account.

Of course, you do not need to do this calculation as your broker does it for you. You simply need to be aware of the types of numbers you are playing with. And if another currency is the counter currency, then pips will be figured in the other currency and converted back, so they won't work out to a whole number of dollars or pounds sterling.

The details of the trades can be left to the computers; what you need to be concerned with is identifying profitable trades, and I discuss various ways to do that later.

Forex Brokers

What can I say? Caveat emptor seems appropriate. Some, maybe many, Forex brokers are very good, and content to make their profit by satisfying the customers. But you need to watch out for the ones that are not so honest, and it can be difficult to work this out from appearances.

First, if you choose a broker in your home country, then they should come under the laws and regulations that you are familiar with, and if they act improperly, it is relatively much easier to pursue them for a resolution. Of course with the power of the Internet, you are at liberty to open an account virtually anywhere, so if you are happy with an overseas broker by all means go ahead. After all, there are legitimate reasons for a broker to want to operate offshore, such as a better climate and perhaps tax advantages; it is just more difficult for you to pursue a legal remedy if necessary.

Nowadays, the quality of the website is no indication of the quality or longevity of the broker's operation. It is easy to think that a well-built functional website means that the broker is well established and vested in a reliable operation. However the price of a professional website, or even of copying an existing website, is low compared to the amount the shyster can expect in fraudulent gains.

Similarly, do not believe everything that a Forex broker states on his site. One fake broker who defrauded a client gave a legitimate sounding US address for his office which turned out to be a residential property in foreclosure. See if you can check with a trade association or the Better Business Bureau on the quality of the operation.

While on the topic of fraud, be aware that the Internet which you rely upon for your information can be manipulated. Checking a broker online is no guarantee, as anyone can say what they want. There was a New York based broker who arranged to get many false favorable posts online, as if from independent traders. Similarly, bad posts about a broker can simply be sour grapes from someone who lost money, and do not mean that the broker is necessarily no good.

Types of Dealing

There are two types of Forex dealing. Some brokers operate a retail side with a dealing desk where they are calling the prices; this is fairly common, and okay if you trust the broker. The other type of dealer allows ECN access direct to the market. ECN stands for electronic communication network. Brokers offering ECN accounts include Dukascopy, M.B.Trading, Currenex, Hotspot, and FXDD.

If the broker offers fixed spreads between the bid and ask prices, you can be fairly sure that he is operating a dealing desk and setting his own prices. Normally the markets would dictate the spreads, as they vary during the day.

The potential problem with the dealing desk is simply that it is open to manipulation. For example, the prices can be manipulated particularly when you're trying to close a winning position. Or if you have a stoploss order which closes your trade at a particular price, then the broker can arrange for the price to be hit, rather than let you win with a profitable position.

Again, this is not to say that all dealing desk operations are to be avoided, just to warn you about some of the shadier tactics that unscrupulous brokers have employed.

Signing Up

The process of signing up for an account is relatively straightforward, although you must be prepared to reveal things that are not required for other memberships. For example, in the US you will need to give out your Social Security number, your banking information, and information about your employment. Generally you need to provide detailed financial information, as well as signing a commitment that you understand the risks involved.

It would be nice to think that these things are required to protect you from doing something rash. However they are in place also to protect the broker from a client who has more optimism than knowledge, and who may have difficulty meeting their commitments should they lose. Inevitably, the broker must protect his interests first and foremost, and is usually legally required to provide at least minimal notices to potential customers of the risks involved.

With the information that you give him, the broker will assess whether you can qualify for an account, and also how much margin or leverage you should be permitted. This often works out to 100 to 1, but just because the broker gives it to you does not mean you need to use it. When you're starting out, 20 to 1 is easily enough. I cover risks in more detail in the Money Management chapter.

Your Account

Once your account is approved, you are able to start Forex trading! If you have only read this far in the book, I would strongly suggest that you do not. As a reminder, more Forex traders lose than win, and some of them have been doing it for a long time. The least you should do is acquaint yourself with the knowledge of the markets in the remainder of this book before dabbling around online.

This doesn't prevent you from downloading any software that your broker offers, and getting familiar with that. Often, it will be MetaTrader 4 or 5, or one of a couple of other software programs that brokers "buy in" to provide for their clients. Occasionally a broker may custom build their own trading platform, but this is unusual.

Sometimes, particularly with the possibility of mobile trading, you will find that there is no software to download and that you simply use your browser, with the dealer's website providing the mechanics.

Incidentally, most if not all brokers provide the facility for you to practice on a "demo" account free of charge, with virtual money. Once you want to start placing trades, you would be foolish not to use this facility first. It is not the same as using real money, as I'll discuss in the Psychology chapter later, but the least it will do is get you familiar with the interface so that you do not make too many mistakes when it comes to real trading.

Technical Analysis

Technical analysis is a huge topic, and one that you may find yourself coming back to again and again during your trading career. You need to understand the basics of technical analysis, but much of it is okay for you to take in only as you need it. For example, there are more than 100 "technical indicators", but most traders will only use two or three of the popular ones that they become familiar with.

If you do other financial trading, you will find that the technical analysis principles apply to stocks, futures, or any other financial instruments. They are based on human nature and psychology, as observed in practice.

For the sake of clarity, this section will be broken down into the following main topics: –

1. The Foundation of Technical Analysis

2. Charting Principles

3. Trends

4. Patterns

5. Moving Averages

6. Indicators

Each of these topics has many subtopics.

Foundations of Technical Analysis

What Is It and Why Should You Care?

Technical analysis is based on "market action", which is all that you can know about a trading market (unless you have insider knowledge). In the case of Forex, it is simply a study of the way the price moves over time. You do not even have the amount of information you can get for stocks of how many shares have been sold, as Forex happens in many different countries and markets and no one has the total picture.

But the fundamental principle of technical analysis is that market action reflects everything there is to know about the price, at a particular moment in time. There are many things that can affect currency prices, including government actions, interest rates, employment and industrial output, etc., and technical analysis cuts across all that by saying that anything that can be known is already included in the price that you see.

In other words, you don't need to bother about the things that move the price, you can just look at the price over time, and everything's included.

Nice idea, makes things a whole lot easier, but does it work? The answer to that is yes, over the years technical analysis has proved itself to work out.

There is one important point to make here. If technical analysis "tells you" that the price is due to go up, then it may or may not go up. The market will always do what it wants, regardless of what it "should" do. What technical analysis provides you with is an indication of the most likely outcome. In other words, using technical analysis simply puts probability on your side. Averaged out over many different trades you hope to make a profit; but you should never bet your house, or a significant amount of money that you cannot afford to lose, on one trade regardless of how many technical pointers suggest its success.

So the first idea of technical analysis is that market action is all you need to analyze prices and improve your chances.

The second idea of technical analysis is that prices tend to move in trends. If a price is going up, it will tend to keep going up until something happens to change that. It's like Newton's laws of motion – a body in motion will stay in motion unless acted upon by an external force.

This again has been shown over time to be true. If it was not, you would never see the charts behaving as they do, but rather a lot of random price movement.

And the third idea is simply that history repeats itself. If you've seen something happen in the past in certain circumstances, then if you see those circumstances again, quite possibly you will see that something happen again. We don't expect people to change, so we expect the same results.

In a nutshell, that's what technical analysis is about. And you should care because it is one of the keys to learning to trade in a way that increases your chances of success.

But What About . . .?

You will hear some arguments against technical analysis. The ultimate proof is that it works, at least to improve your percentages, but here is what some people say about technical analysis.

Charts only show what has happened in the past, how can they reveal what hasn't happened yet?

Well, we have evidence from many years of trading that technical analysis can work. The third idea that history repeats itself asserts that you can anticipate, to some extent, what is going to happen. After all, do you ever listen to the weather forecast in the morning to see whether to take your umbrella to work? See, you already believe that past events can be interpreted to predict the future!

If the prices already incorporate everything there is to know, then any change in price can only come from new information that we don't know yet.

This idea surfaces in various forms in all financial markets, and is still discussed by academics. Contrary to popular opinion this idea does not even say that the current price is correct, simply that there is no way to know if it is too high or too low.

The best way to refute this idea is to demonstrate that technical analysis does work. After all, if everyone believed it then no one would do any analysis, and the price would never change.

Technical analysis is self-fulfilling. If everyone analyzes the chart and decides the price should go up, then they will all buy, and the increased demand will make the price go up. The same argument applies to the price going down.

No wonder technical analysis works so well! Seriously, so what? There is probably some truth in this, but who cares why if the price goes in the direction that you anticipate? The fact that the majority of would-be traders fail to make a profit suggests that the idea of traders operating "en masse" is somewhat mistaken.

Charting Principles

Now it is time to look at charting, or graphing of the prices, and what it all means. You cannot run away from this, as it is a fundamental to your trading. It is not so difficult to understand, as long as you take it step-by-step.

There are several different types of chart, but most of them use a timescale along the horizontal bottom of the chart, and the price up the side. These are the only types you need to know. The timescale can vary from minutes to days or weeks, and which of these you look at depends on your style of trading – though you usually want to see what's happening on different time scales around your chosen values, just to get the big picture.

Here are three types of charts, all for the same currency and time. They are the line chart, bar chart, and candlestick chart.

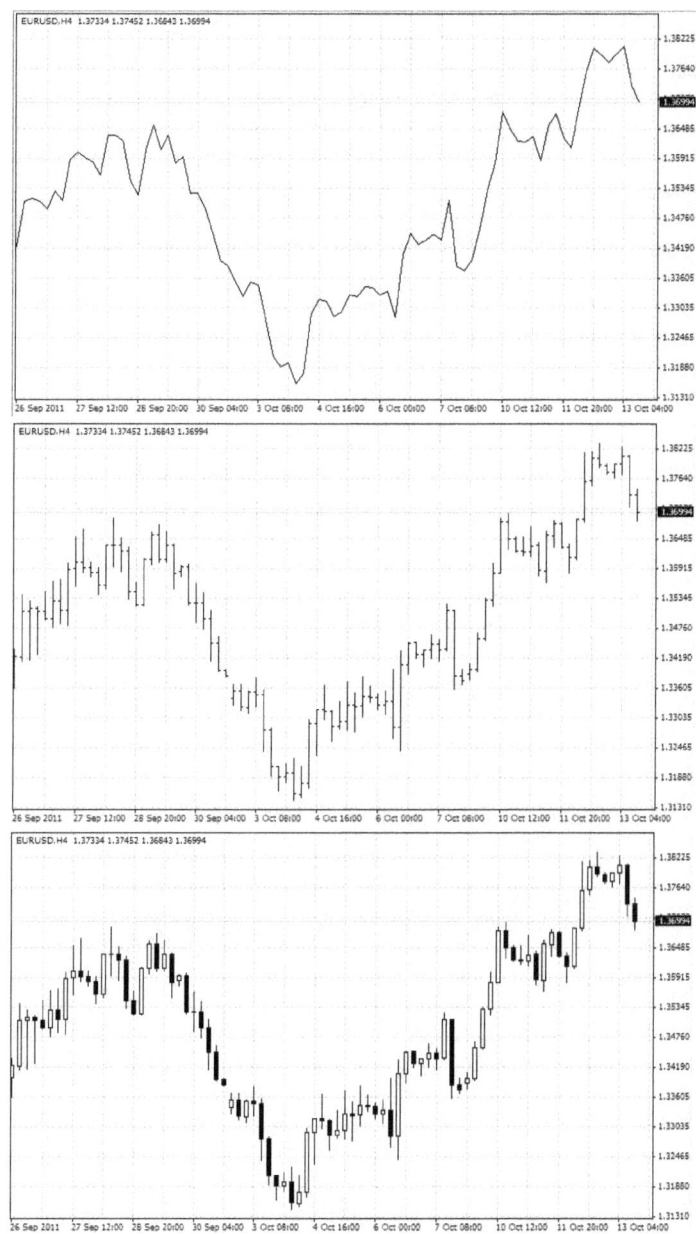

These charts may be a little difficult to read, so they (and all other diagrams in this book) are available online at www.newbiesguidetoforex.com, or go to any freely available charting service such as sharpcharts.com or bigcharts.com and pull up similar charts.

The first chart, the line chart, contains less information than the other two. It only plots the closing price for each time period, and joins them together with the line. You won't use that one much. But both the bar chart and the candlestick chart show exactly the same information, and most traders prefer the candlestick chart as the information is easier to understand at a glance.

You will recall that all we know about a price is called "market action". Looking at the candlestick chart, each one of those vertical "candles" as they are called includes a four hour period, as this one happens to be a four-hour chart. And there are four different prices plotted for each period. The prices are the lowest value, the highest value, the opening price (at the start of the period), and the closing price (at the end of the trading period).

To show this information clearly, the Japanese invented this candlestick charting method, which has only been known about and used in the West for a few decades. Prior to that, everyone had to use the bar chart. The way the individual bars show four prices is illustrated on the next page.

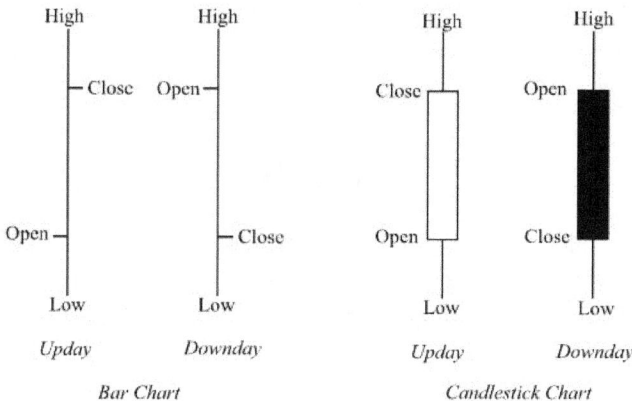

Here you can see the cleverness of the candlestick method. While the bar chart just puts little lines, called tics, each side of the vertical bar at the levels of the opening and closing prices, the candle actually changes color depending whether it is an up day or a down day. This is much easier to spot on a chart.

The fat part of the candle is called the "real body", and is shown in white for an uptrend and black for a downtrend above, a common standard. You may see it green and red, and may even be able to set it in your charting program to colors that you prefer. It is just important that you can see at a glance whether the price for the time period finished up or finished down overall.

Having now established the reasons to prefer candlestick charting, that is the only sort of charting I will show in the rest of this book. It is only a tool, so feel free to use another method if you wish, the same principles will apply.

Trends

Again a fundamental idea, trends indicate whether the price is generally going up or going down. Markets trend about 40% of the time, the rest of the time they float around the same level, which is known as "sideways" movement or range trading, and you'll see later that there are different strategies to use depending on what the market is doing.

To get the definition out of the way, uptrends are when the price makes higher and higher peaks, and higher and higher troughs or low points. Downtrends are when the troughs get lower and lower, and so do the price peaks. As you can see from the previous charts, prices don't just go straight up or down in a trend, but wiggle around. So the right side of the chart shows an erratic but definite uptrend, and this follows on from a fairly smooth downtrend to the left.

While trends are fundamental to analysis, you must be careful not to get too hung up on the definition. It all depends on your point of view. For instance, taken on a larger time frame the chart we just looked at could simply be an uptrend. Or you could chop the uptrend on the right into smaller parts, and see several different uptrends interspersed with downtrends. Make sure you relate your observation of a trend to the time period you are trading over.

Support and Resistance

Support and resistance are price levels that the price seems reluctant to go beyond. Support is a level below the market price, and if the price goes down to it, it may reverse and go back up. Resistance is above the current price, and the price may go up to it then back down.

When you see support and/or resistance working like that, it seems almost magical. Of course, ultimately either may be broken, but they can be "hit" many times before they concede.

Some basic points about support and resistance. The more times they have been hit, and the price has bounced back, the more they can be trusted. The further back in time you go, finding the same levels, the stronger they should prove to be. When either of them fails, and the price significantly penetrates past, then the level reverses its role – for instance, if the price pushes up through a resistance then on its next retracement down it may well stop at the same level, using it as a support.

Traditionally, support and resistance are thought of as being at set levels, actual prices, and often, because of the psychology of it, they will occur at whole numbers such as 10, 20, 1.500 – just something that looks significant.

Trends and Channels

There is another type of support and resistance, and that is known as the "trendline" and its "channel line". A trend line is sloping, for example in an uptrend it slopes upward and connects successive rising market bottoms. In a downtrend, it slopes downwards and connects successive falling market peaks.

The channel line is drawn as a line parallel to the trendline, on the opposite side of the price. Here's a chart to show what I mean.

Again this is taken from the previous chart, just looking at the uptrend portion. As it is an uptrend, the trendline is the lower one, drawn to connect the troughs or bottoms in price. The channel line is the upper parallel line; spaced far enough away that it connects the peaks.

The channel provides price support and resistance which changes over time, as you can see. In this example, on the far right, you will see there is a candle that has gone below the trendline. This is just the sort of thing that you can look for. While these lines are not set in stone, and the price will not always accurately touch them before reversing, it's quite possible that the break below the line signifies the end of the trend and a start of range trading (the price trading in a set range) or even a downtrend. Finding out things like this early will help your trading.

Patterns

This is the first section on patterns, and covers the general shape of the price line on the chart. This is traditional Western-style technical analysis. A later section covers candlestick patterns, which reference the appearance of each candlestick with several candlesticks making up the pattern.

Reversal Patterns

Much of the time you will be looking for reversal patterns, which indicates that a reversal in the trend is imminent. If you can see when the price will reverse its direction, obviously you are able to make money out of this.

Head and Shoulders

If you have studied any financial trading you're probably familiar with the Head and Shoulders Pattern, which is also perhaps the most reliable of the Western reversal patterns. This pattern is made up of three market peaks, with the middle peak or head a little higher than the adjacent peaks. It comes in an uptrend and suggests a reversal into a downtrend.

Here's a chart showing a head and shoulders reversal pattern. You can see that I drew a trendline, and then tried to complete the channel. The channel line did not work because some prices pushed above it, and sometimes they do not. I left it in as an example, to show you that you cannot expect "copy book" charts all the time.

But the head and shoulders pattern is to the right, with three peaks, the middle one being the higher "head". You can draw a line across the shoulders, as I have here, and this is called the neckline.

A couple of points. The two shoulder peaks will always be lower than the head, but it does not matter which one is above the other. Often, the neckline will slope up slightly, such as in this case, but it can be either way. The head and shoulders pattern is considered confirmed once the price drops decisively through the neckline.

If you think about it, you will see that the head and shoulders pattern is nothing special, just a description of an uptrend faltering and what you might expect to see on the price chart.

Inverse Head and Shoulders

This is a note to say that you can see a head and shoulders pattern upside down at the end of a downtrend, when it would signify a reversal to an uptrend. The same descriptions apply.

Double and Tripled Tops and Bottoms

These patterns are similar to the head and shoulders, but as the name suggests consist of two or three peaks or troughs, rather than having the "head" sticking out further. Basically, the lack of further progress of the trend, with the peaks only going up to the same level as previously, suggests that the trend is **weakening**. The trend is considered reversed once the price starts going back down. Common sense.

Continuation Patterns

Usually continuation patterns occur and the price keeps on going in the direction that it was going previously. These are in effect consolidation before a further push.

Triangles

These can give you good information about the price progress. Usually the triangle is narrowing over time, squeezing down the range of price until it cannot be contained any longer and breaks out. As such, you can get clear indications of dramatic moves.

Look at the ascending triangle for example: –

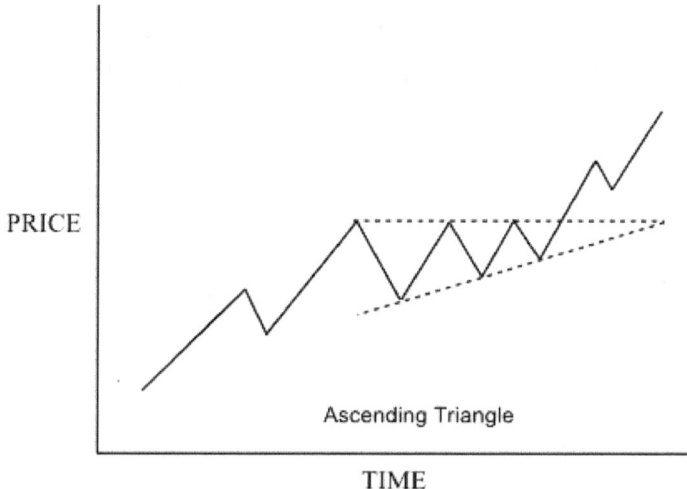

PRICE

Ascending Triangle

TIME

This usually occurs in an uptrend, as shown, and consists of the price banging away at a resistance level, being repeatedly rebuffed, until finally it breaks through. Basically you are following the progress of the price as it bounces between two converging trendlines, and the price will break out between half and three quarters of the way along the triangle.

If you think about what is going on here, the buyers are pushing the price up to the top line repeatedly, and then the sellers are taking over, letting the price go back down. The buyers keep going all the way up to the resistance level, the sellers are weakening, take the price back down less each time, so it is no surprise that eventually the price breaks out upwards.

Of course, you can also have a descending triangle which is usually in a downtrend.

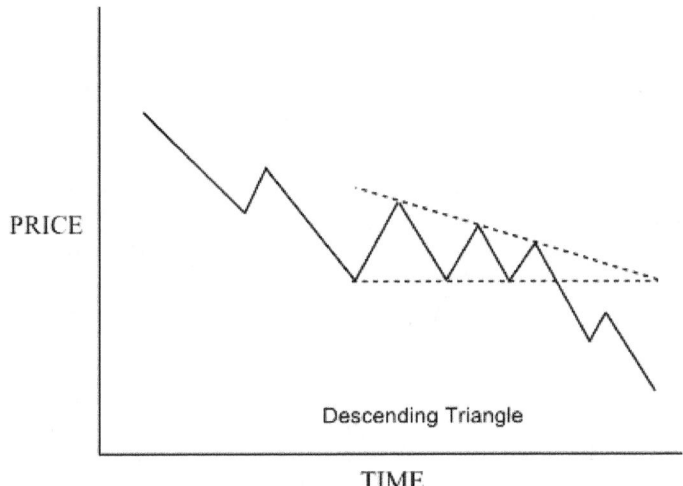

PRICE

Descending Triangle

TIME

Similar arguments apply to the reasons for this.

Note this is not to say that you won't see those triangles in the opposite trend, or to say that the price will always go up from an ascending triangle and down from a descending triangle. These are just the likely configurations, ones you'll see more often than not.

You can also get what is called a symmetrical triangle, where the upper line slopes downwards and the lower line slopes up.

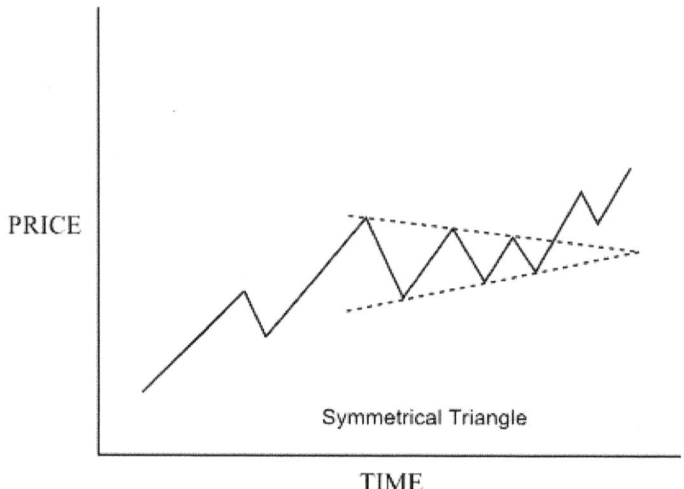

PRICE

Symmetrical Triangle

TIME

This is often just a pausing point in a trend which continues afterwards, and you can see it in an uptrend or a downtrend.

The feature with all these triangles is that you reach a point where the price must be resolved, because the price range it is oscillating within is getting smaller and smaller. Once the price breaks out of the triangle, you have a fair idea that it will continue in that direction.

I should just mention one other type of triangle. This is different from the rest, and is called a Broadening Formation. It's also sometimes called a Megaphone Top. It's the opposite type of triangle, with the trendlines opening outwards or broadening as time passes. This shows a chaotic time in the market, with prices swinging more and more wildly. You're most likely to see this in an uptrend with it followed by a downtrend, but as the action is so wild you're best not to risk trading in this situation.

Flag and Rectangle

The flag and the rectangle are similar patterns, both showing oscillation between two parallel lines. Here's the flag in an uptrend: –

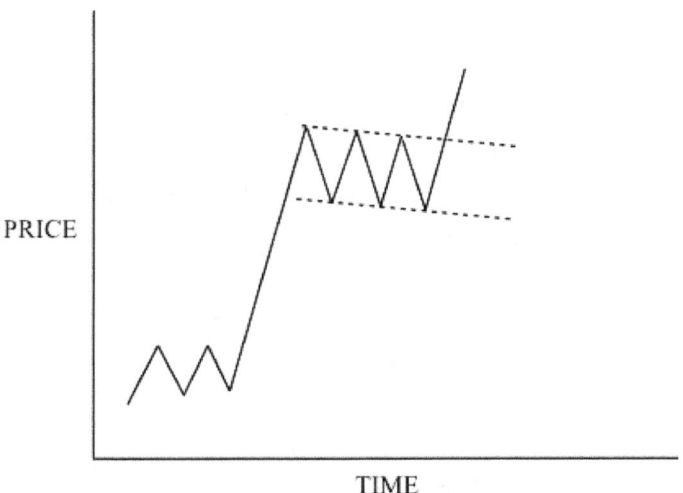

and here's the rectangle: –

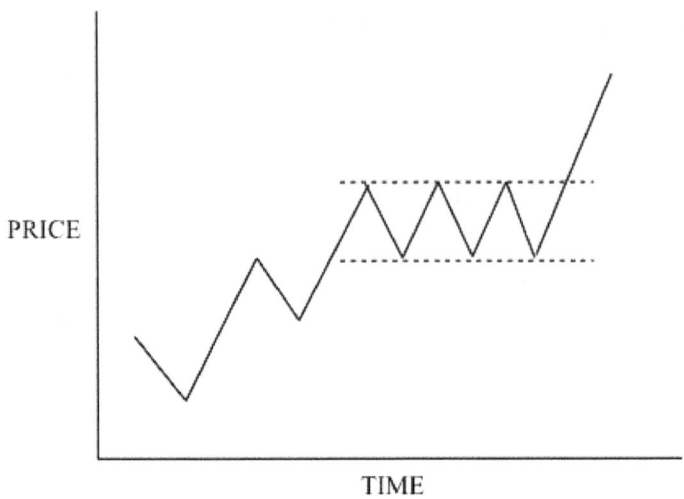

These are normally continuation patterns, though as with all trading there are exceptions. The flag in particular will often come after a sharp move, and it is almost as if the market has to catch its breath, consolidating for a few weeks, before continuing the trend. Usually the flag is sloped countertrend.

Moving Averages

The moving average is one of the most widely used indicators in trading, and also one of the most versatile. It can be applied in several different ways, and is easy to understand, making it a very popular tool for the technical analyst.

One difference from pattern recognition methods is that a moving average is unambiguous, and you do not need to interpret it in any way, which means you can reliably test on historic information any trading system you devise.

Simple Moving Average (SMA)

Most people are familiar with the idea of an average. You simply take X numbers, add them all together, and divide by X to get the average number. So the average of one, three, six, and eight is 1+3+6+8 divided by four, the number of numbers, which works out to 4.5.

In trading, the simple moving average is calculated in the same way, using X prices up to and including today to get the value for today. So an SMA (5), as it is written, would take the price from each of the last five trading sessions to get the value for today. Each session's simple moving average value is connected to form a continuous graph. Here's an example with the chart we used earlier: –

This is an SMA (14), which means it combines the 14 previous prices and averages them for each trading period. As you can see, because of the way it is made it lags the price action, playing catch-up all the time. The general term for this is "lagging indicator".

It tends to smooth out price action, and shows you the direction of the trend as it develops. In fact, depending on the value of the SMA, it can act like a curving trend line, marking out support or resistance levels.

As the value gets smaller, the line follows the price more closely. The larger the value, the more the moving average tends to smooth out the price information.

Exponential Moving Average (EMA)

Different but similar to the SMA, the exponential moving average was invented to try and eliminate some of the time lag, and make the line more relevant to the current price.

There are other types of moving average, such as the weighted moving average, the triangular moving average, the variable moving average, etc. all with their own particular techniques of combining recent prices to try and make them more accurate for future projections.

Single Moving Average

One of the simplest methods to see when to trade is using a single moving average. You plot the moving average on your chart, and when the price crosses it, you take that as a signal.

As the price is more recent than the moving average, if the price crosses above then that is bullish, if below it is bearish. You can try different types of moving average, and different numbers of periods.

You can see how this might have worked on the chart above. The most obvious trade is when the price drops below the moving average about a quarter of the way across. Around the middle of the chart, the price rises above, which would signify a long trade, but as you can see this did not go anywhere. Two other times when the price rises up through the moving average, you would have made some profit.

What you made would have depended on how you decided to close the trades. If you waited for the price to recross the moving average, you might lose most of the gains. I will talk about different trade exits later.

You can refine the system, and play around with it using different numbers and types of moving average, and see how it would perform. It is very simple, not great, but I'm sure you can see some possibilities.

Two Moving Averages

Another way to find a trading signal is to plot two moving averages, each based on a different time period. Here, you trade when the moving averages cross each other. You can see it's the same idea as above, just a little smoothed out – after all, the price itself is simply a version of a hypothetical SMA(1).

Common pairs to use it might include a 5 and a 20, a 10 and a 50. It is really up to you to try out to find what works best. Trying out the 5 and 20 on our chart:-

Over by the left edge, the moving averages cross, calling for a long trade. A quarter of the way across they cross again for a short trade, then in the middle another long trade is indicated. In this example, they seem to work pretty well even if you wait for the crossing back before you close your trade.

Once again, you can try different numbers and different types of moving average to refine the performance. With moving average crossings, you get a clear and unambiguous signal of when to trade, so you can apply this method consistently.

Bollinger Bands

Bollinger Bands are a refinement on moving averages, and again have several uses. They are plotted as three lines, the center one being a moving average and the ones above and below spaced according to how volatile the price is, usually at "two standard deviations", if you understand statistical terms.

What this means is that the bands will get tighter or further apart depending how much the price is fluctuating. Here's our sample chart.

You can see that the bands tend to contain the price, opening out when the price is moving a lot, and closing up when the price is steady. Statisticians tell us that "two standard deviations" should contain about 95% of the price movement.

Often the price will tend to follow the band, but seldom penetrating it. You can see this in a downtrend on the left, when the band acts as a source of support. On the right of the chart, the movement is more erratic but the price is still seems to be hitting resistance every time it reaches the upper band.

Some traders take it as a change of trend when the price crosses the middle line, and then the opposite band becomes a price target. Certainly the middle line can seem to be a support or resistance to the movement of the price, as you can see in the uptrend on the right.

In other words, if you're in an uptrend then the price will probably fluctuate between the middle and the upper band; in a downtrend the price will be between the middle and lower band. If it strays far away from this guideline, then you are probably looking at a change of trend.

Just one more point of note for Bollinger Bands. If the distance between the bands becomes narrow, it often means that the price is about to break out and start a new trend. It's as though the price is being throttled right down until it can't be contained any more.

Indicators

By now you should be feeling some of the excitement of trading, seeing how it is possible to anticipate, to some extent, where the price is going, which gives you the possibility of making profitable trades. But you're still at the early stages, so don't let your enthusiasm run away with you until you have seen what else is to come.

This section deals with indicators, which are lines or values which are calculated from the price action, and may provide better indications of future market sentiment and the price movement.

There are many different indicators, and more being invented all the time to overcome perceived shortcomings of the existing ones. Many traders stick with just two or three established indicators, and it's really not necessary to use many on a day-to-day basis.

I include in this section oscillators, which term describes indicators which go between limits, or oscillate, usually to show when the market is "oversold" or "overbought". The theory is that if the market is oversold, too many people have sold out of it and it is due for people to buy back in when they think about it. Effectively, the price is lower than it should be. If the market is overbought, there's been a rush of enthusiasm which has pushed the price up too far, so you might expect the price to pull back soon.

From a practical point of view, many oscillators are plotted separately beneath the chart. I give the derivation of the indicators in the descriptions, but in practice your computer will take care of any figuring out and plotting, so don't worry if any sound too complicated. You should however have some idea of where the indicator is getting its information, as when you use a second indicator for confirmation of a signal it should be based on different parameters.

Moving Average Convergence-Divergence (MACD)

Although it looks slightly more complicated than many of the oscillators you will see later, I start with this one as we have just been talking about moving averages. It is a well-known and much used indicator. The abbreviation MACD is usually pronounced "mac-dee".

The MACD is plotted below the regular chart, as shown. I have added a couple of moving averages to the chart so that you can follow the derivation of the MACD, but usually you would not need to do this.

The MACD starts by plotting the difference between two exponential moving averages, the EMA (12) and the EMA (26) usually, although you can put in what values you want. These are the moving averages I have put on the chart, and as you can see the difference is plotted with the bars in the indicator below.

As we saw before, you can take the crossing of two moving averages as a signal to buy or to sell, and it usually tends to lag behind the price action. The MACD is the plot of the difference, so when it is zero that is the same as the average lines crossing, as you can see. So far, this is another way of showing what we looked at before.

The signal line is a plot of the moving average of the MACD value. This has the effect of showing how the original exponential moving averages are converging and diverging, and this means it can anticipate the converging, or crossing, and give an earlier signal.

There are several pieces of information that we can get from the MACD indicator. When the signal line goes below the bars that can be used as a buy signal and when the signal line goes above the MACD bars it is a sell signal.

As the MACD goes above and below zero, it acts as an oscillator showing overbought and oversold conditions. When the MACD is high above zero, it indicates overbought or a good time to sell; when the MACD is well below zero, it shows oversold or a good time to buy.

The MACD shown is that plotted with MetaTrader 4, from which all these examples are plotted. Some charting programs show the MACD plotted simply as a line, rather than using vertical bars. The same analysis applies.

Relative Strength Index (RSI)

Another popular indicator is the relative strength index, invented about three decades ago. This looks at the price performance over a previous number of periods, in this case 14, and compares the number of up days and down days to get an idea of the momentum of the market in either direction.

In brief, if the RSI goes below 30% then comes back up through it, is taken as a buying signal; if the RSI is above 70% and drops down below that, it may be a selling signal. The signal is when the value comes back towards the middle, not when it reaches that level.

Stochastic Oscillator

The stochastic oscillator was invented by Dr. Lane, and in the 1990s was used extensively by traders because of its effectiveness. One reason for this may be because it considers more of the price action than many other oscillators.

The stochastic oscillator considers where the closing price is in relation to the total price range for the time period. Simply put, in an uptrend you might expect the closing price to be near the top of the range, and in a downtrend near the bottom.

It's an interesting fact that Lane was experimenting with many different indicators at the time, and that is the historic reason that the lines have strange names – %K for the solid line and %D for the dotted line.

In its simplest form, when the solid line crosses up through the dotted line, that's a bullish signal, and when it drops down through the indication is bearish. You usually wait until the lines are in "overextended" territory, which is above 80 or below 20 as shown on this chart (and some traders use 75 and 25).

As this is a much more active indicator than the RSI, it can give too many signals, telling you to trade too frequently. Many traders use the RSI together with the stochastic oscillator, as the RSI is less volatile and would not trigger your trades so often.

Indicator Use

You will find many other oscillators on your charting program. The ones shown above are just a few that are on MetaTrader 4. The interpretation is usually similar. An oscillator can give you early warning of a potential change, and at extreme values can indicate that a correction is due, but usually only when it starts coming back to the center – oscillator values can stay high or stay low for a time, and there's no change in the price action.

Another point to watch with oscillators is that they usually go up and down mirroring the price. Any time they go in the opposite direction to the price is usually a "watch out" time, and you can expect changes to happen.

Candlestick Patterns

Candlestick charts were introduced to the Western world in the 1980s, but have been used for centuries in Japan, where they originated. As mentioned previously, they show exactly the same information as the Western-style bar chart, but because of the use of solid bodies the information is much easier to comprehend at a glance.

To recap, the overall length of the candle, from wick to wick, is the entire trading range for the time in question; the fat part, or body, shows the distance between the opening price and the closing price, with the color showing you whether it finished higher or lower for the period.

The overall length of the candle shows how volatile the price has been, whereas the length of the real body shows how much progress the price has made over the whole day. If the body is short, then the opening and closing prices are very similar, which is usually interpreted as the sellers and the buyers being in balance; if it is a long body, that tends to show that one side is much stronger than the other, moving the price decisively.

Types of Candles

This is a special candle, called a Doji. The real body is just a horizontal line, which means that the opening and closing prices were exactly the same. The Japanese place great importance on the Doji. It shows complete balance between the sellers and buyers, and thus is often thought of as a sign that a trend is reversing.

Note that the horizontal line can be anywhere on the wick, at the top or the bottom or in the middle as shown.

These are regular candles, but with fairly short bodies and with long wicks, and may be referred to as "high wave" candles.

The meaning is similar to the Doji.

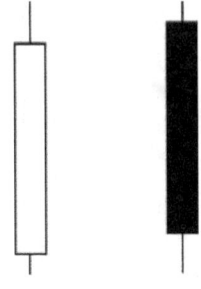

These candles have long bodies, which tends to suggest that a trend is strong. You can also get candles without any wicks, and they are called Marubozu. They indicate that there was no trading outside the range of the opening to the closing price, and that's a very strong indication as the market was pushing in one direction only.

Candlestick patterns can be one or more candles long, and usually indicate a reversal although there are patterns that suggest a continuation. The interpretations build on the ideas such as long wicks or long bodies show strength, and short ones shown indecisiveness.

In almost every case, the pattern's interpretation depends on there being a prior trend and on its direction.

Hammer

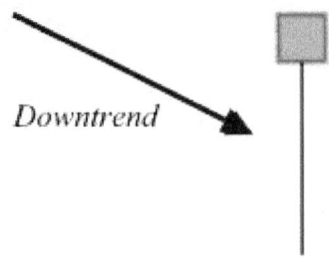

Downtrend

The ideal Hammer candlestick signal has a small body and a lower wick at least twice the length of the body. It does not matter if the day was up or down, which is why I have shown the body as grey.

The hammer may signal a trend reversal, which would be confirmed and actionable if the following day the price started going up.

It works because the price has been going down for time, and some traders start panicking and want to sell at any price, pushing down the wick. But smart money comes in and starts buying, pushing the price back up at the close. The reversal during the day may continue the following day.

Hanging Man

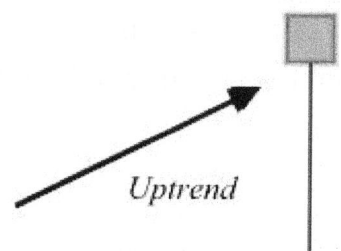

Uptrend

The Hanging Man looks the same, but comes in an uptrend. Again you would look for a change of trend on the following day to confirm the reversal.

In this case the psychology is that many traders decide to take profits, pushing the price down, but some novices see this as an opportunity to buy, pushing the price back up at the close. However, as this is a weak candle, on reflection traders feel that the trend is finished and selling increases on the following days.

Inverted Hammer

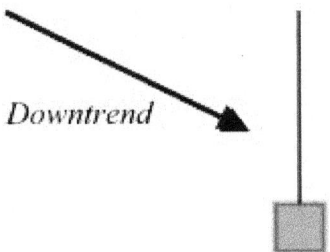

Downtrend

You can see from the diagram that this is very similar to the last two candlestick patterns. The psychology of this signaling a reversal is as follows.

The downtrend is weakening, and some traders are having second thoughts, buying in which pushes the price up. The sellers come back in so the price closes down, but if the price starts going up on the following day, then the perceived weakness makes more traders buy, pushing the price up, and starting an uptrend.

Shooting Star

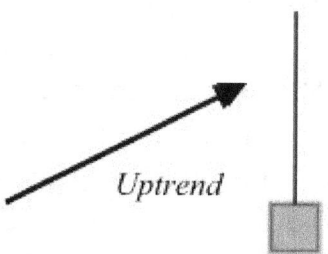

The last of this set of four related single candle signals, the Shooting Star comes in an uptrend. It is well-known that novices always buy at the top, and this simply demonstrates that. The exuberance that causes the high wick is noticed by other traders who decided it must be time to sell. Once again, you need to see what happens on the following day to make sure that it truly signals a reversal.

Bullish Engulfing

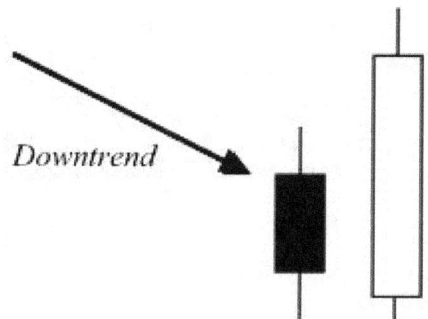

This is a high probability two candle pattern. In a downtrend, on the first candle the selling pressure continues, so much so that the following candle opens at an even lower price. But smart money has identified an opportunity, and plows in to buy on the second candle, sending the price up above the previous period. This shows that the strength is with the buyers, and that the reversal is likely.

Bearish Engulfing

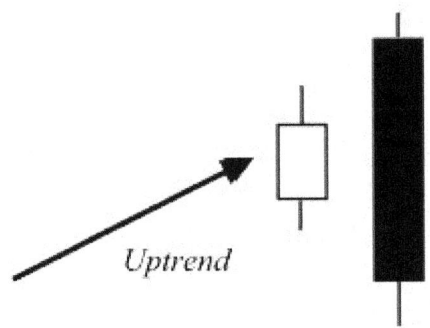

Uptrend

Exactly the same idea as the bullish pattern. The uptrend stretches so hard, with an opening price even higher than the previous candle, that smart people decide it might be a good time to sell. The length of the black candle shows that the weight of opinion is behind the reverse to a downtrend.

Piercing Candle

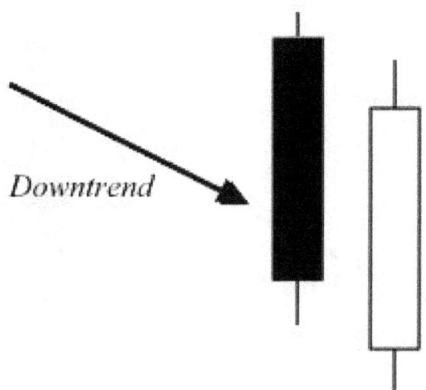

Downtrend

This pattern shows a strong bearish candle in a downtrend, with the following candle opening at an even lower price but rallying to finish in the previous day's trading range.

It works as a reversal signal because the first candle indicates that traders selling are reaching a hopeless state. With the price drop even lower, the smart money moves in and starts buying strongly enough to push the price up.

Dark Cloud Cover

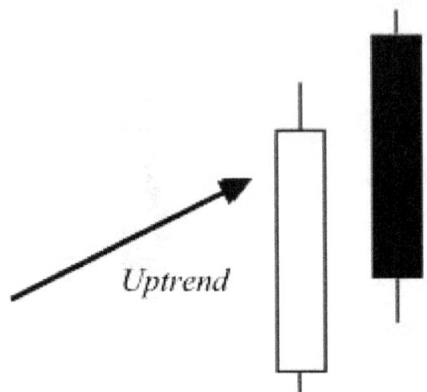

The Dark Cloud Cover is similar to the Piercing formation, but in an uptrend.

Bullish Harami

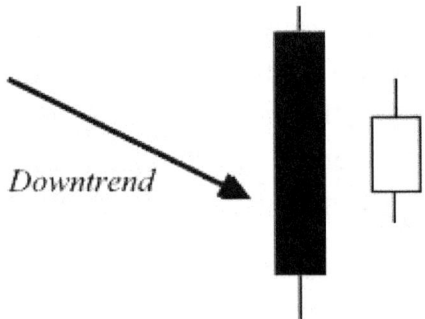

The Japanese word Harami means "pregnant", and they obviously thought that this candlestick pattern looks like a pregnant woman.

In this scenario, there's been a lot of selling, but the second candlestick shows the price opened higher. Buying pressure means that the second candle finishes up, and this can signal a reversal. Again, it is wise to see what happens on the following day.

Bearish Harami

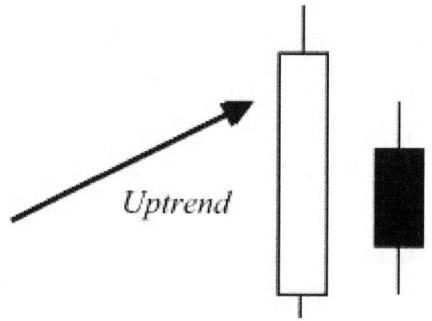

Coming at the end of an uptrend, the first candlestick shows naïve exuberance. When the second period opens at a lower price and continues down during the day, it indicates that the buyers have had second thoughts. It is quite likely that the selling will continue and resolve into a downtrend.

Candlestick Rules

There are many other named candlestick patterns that you will find in books, but these are the main ones that you may choose to remember. There are even some software programs that identify the patterns on a price chart for you.

However, you should never consider trading on the basis of finding a candlestick pattern alone. First and foremost, the pattern needs to occur in the right trend to have any validity. Secondly, you should look for indicators or other reasons that a reversal may be expected.

If you have agreement between Western indicators and candlesticks then the reversal is more likely. Even then, it is often a good practice to wait until the following time period to make sure that the price sets off in the direction you expect.

Fundamental Analysis

Traders usually refer to technical analysis in order to time their short term trading. Fundamentals as applied to stocks and shares seldom have much to do with the timing of price moves, but merely the overall value that companies can be expected to achieve at some stage.

When you are trading on the Forex market, however, there are many fundamental factors that can rapidly impact the exchange rates. Governments routinely issue statistics that affect how their country's currency is viewed, and you need to be aware of when these announcements are made so that you do not get caught out, or can take advantage of them if appropriate.

You should note that news is often factored into prices before it is announced. Hence when the announcements actually come, you may not see much movement and you can even see price movement in the opposite direction to what you would expect. As in all trading, you have to act on what you can observe, and not what you may expect. Here are some of the factors which tend to influence exchange rates.

US Non-Farm Payrolls

This is a measure of the number of jobs created outside the farming industry, which is historically discounted because it tends to be seasonal. The economy is considered to be doing better when more jobs are created. At the same time, the related unemployment rate is issued.

Obviously, strong figures here are good for the US dollar, and should strengthen it against other currencies. Poor figures suggest a weaker dollar.

US Federal Reserve

The Feds announce interest rates eight times a year, when the Federal Open Market Committee meets. Right now there's not a lot they can do with interest rates, because the rates are so low, but usually they have more flexibility and can impact the US dollar exchange rates.

When the interest rate goes up, that strengthens the dollar's position because it attracts more investors into the US dollar. If the interest rate goes down, that can weaken the dollar.

US Trade Balance

Despite the growth of China, the size of the US consumer market is a major factor in world trade. Because it is a consumer oriented market, usually the US balance of payments is negative, with the US importing more than it exports. In fact you may have seen recently that the cumulative trade deficit is a hot political issue.

It may be that custom and practice will change, but at the moment it is reasonable to expect a negative trade balance. The amount is published every two months, about the middle of the month. The important fact is how much it has changed from the previous numbers, and how different it is from expectations. If the trade balance for the period is less negative, then this is good for the US dollar.

Other US News

The three mentioned above tend to be the most important influencers of the value of the dollar. There are many more factors that can be taken into account. Some of the less influential but still significant news for the market include: –

- Gross Domestic Product

- Consumer Price Inflation

- Retail Sales

- US Treasuries Sales, particularly abroad.

European Factors

If you are trading in a currency pair that includes the US dollar (which includes all six of the most traded currency pairs), then you can expect those factors mentioned above to be very important because of the size of the US economy. But you cannot consider the US economy in isolation, and here are some other items that you should keep an eye on.

Current Account

This is the name for the European equivalent of the trade balance, which is net exports minus net imports. This is usually published at the end of each month, and the significant factor is how much it changes from month to month, rather than the absolute value.

Unemployment Data

For Europe, this is usually published about the 10th of each month. The most important issue is what the current sentiment is, and where observers expect the numbers to be compared with where they finish up.

ZEW Indicator of Economic Sentiment

Published by the Centre for European Economic Research (ZEW) every month, this report includes not only European sentiment but also factors for other countries such as Japan, the UK, France, and Italy. With trading, the overall mood or sentiment is one of the most important factors, and this report allows you to easily see in what direction it is going.

Once again, it is changes from expectation and from previous results that are more significant than the absolute values reported. The previous results are already fully accounted for in the markets, therefore the currency exchange rates will respond mainly to differences from the last results.

Intermarket Relationships

Nothing works in isolation, and this world is increasingly becoming interconnected. Therefore it is natural that we can find some factors which give an indication of other expectations.

Commodity Currencies

It may be obvious, but the Australian dollar, the Canadian dollar, and the New Zealand dollar, which are all referred to as commodity currencies, tend to follow commodity prices. This is because these countries are all rich in resources, so effectively become wealthier if commodity prices rise.

As an aside, and in contrast, the euro, the Swiss franc, and the British pound may be referred to as savings currencies, with a tendency to follow the strength of savings in the market.

The Yen

If you want to trade the USDJPY (US dollar and the Japanese yen), then you should keep an eye on the Japanese stock market and in particular the Nikkei 225 index. You will find that they tend to go up and down together.

The Nikkei 225 index is full of exporting companies such as Canon, Sony, Toyota, and many others. These companies do their best business when the value of the Japanese yen goes down, and therefore the products can be more cheaply imported into other countries.

Because the US dollar is first in the currency pair USDJPY, if the yen is weak against the dollar the value of this Forex pair increases. Therefore, the USDJPY and the Nikkei 225 index will go up and down together.

Gold

You will find that gold and the US dollar show a strong negative correlation, almost always moving in opposite directions. As gold is priced in US dollars in international trade, if the US dollar declines then inevitably the price of gold must go up. So if you are trading the EURUSD (euro against the US dollar) you will find it positively related to the price of gold. A weak dollar makes the EURUSD go up.

You will find the same relationship between the Australian dollar and gold, which prices tend to track each other. This has the additional influence that Australia is commodity rich, as mentioned in the first relationship.

Money Management

No matter how much you have learned about technical analysis, or how many economic reports you consume, unless you master money management you will probably fail. Money management is all about making the right size trades so that you will be able to continue trading even when you have losses.

Losing

I will start with the obvious fact that you will lose some of your trades. Things seldom go as planned, and this was never so true as in the world of financial trading. If you are the type who worries about any losses, and can't get over them, then trading isn't for you. But what you should consider is that on average for half of your trades the market will go in the direction you pick. All you have to do is make sure that each of your losing trades costs you less than each of your winning trades makes you, and then you'll have a profit.

Just to make it clear, the point is not that you make 80% or more winning trades, because you will probably find that impossible, given the uncertain nature of the markets. The point is that you limit your losses on those trades that unfortunately go the wrong way, and make the best of your winning trades – "Cut your losses, and let your winners run" – as the old traders' adage goes.

Percentages

"Lies, damn lies, and statistics" – you may have seen it before, but the point needs emphasizing. If you lose a certain percentage of your funds, you have to make a greater percentage to get back to where you started.

For instance, say you lose 25% of your trading capital. If you only make up 25% on the remainder, you finish up with less than 94% of your original stake. You need to earn 33 1/3% just to get back to the start.

The more you lose, the harder it gets. If you lose 33 1/3% of your stake, then you have to earn 50%. If you lose 50%, then you have to double or make 100% on the remainder **just to get back to where you started**.

And surely the point is not to simply stay where you're at, but to make a profit?

The way to counter the effect of this is to make sure that each trade you place can only lose a small part of your fortune. It would not be uncommon to lose three or four in a row, and if you trade for any length of time then you might expect to see six or seven losses in a row from time to time. If you are risking as much as 10% or even 5% with each trade, you are in danger of having a major setback to your account.

Cutting to the point, many traders would say that you should not risk more than 2% on any one trade. This may sound small, but it comes from experience.

Note that this is how much you risk losing. It depends what sort of trading you're doing how this relates to your stake. For instance, if you are an options trader, you could lose your entire stake if the option does not work out. That's in contrast to someone like a stock trader who can see the value go down, close the trade, and get some money back. Incidentally, although options can become valueless, you can usually trade them on before that happens, so again it depends on your trading strategy.

From a practical point of view, you will need to assess how bad your trade could be, and decide in advance when you are going to exit the trade and cut your losses. Working back from that, you can figure how big a stake you can afford.

Related Trades

You must watch out for related trades, which are ones that usually move together, because in effect you are risking more if you work the 2% rule on each separate trade. Perhaps you could be involved in several currency pairs that involve the US dollar. You have to think what would happen if the dollar decided to move against you – would all your 2% losses happen together, giving you say a 10% loss? Or are some of your trades for the dollar and some against, depending what the other currency is?

Don't Try To Make a Profit

This heading is intended to capture your attention, as it is an important point. In the section above I asked if the point was to make a profit. The answer is obviously yes. However, this should not be your focus.

If you are obsessing about making a profit, you may well do stupid things like "doubling down" after a run of losses, changing your strategies the moment they don't seem to be working, etc. Instead, you should obsess about preserving your capital, and not losing too much.

The fact is that a proven and good trading plan, implemented steadily, is your best chance of making a profit. What you must concentrate on is trading well, and with a reasonable amount of good fortune the profit will come. When you trade well, whatever the outcome of an individual trade, you should congratulate yourself that you stuck to your plan. There is more on this in the next chapter, on discipline.

Types of Order

There are many different types of trading orders, some appropriate to other financial securities, and some only available from particular brokers. The ones you are likely to see with Forex trading include the market order, the limit order, and the stop order.

Market Order

The market order tells your broker to buy or sell at the current price. The order will take place as soon as the broker gets around to it, which for most brokers is almost instantaneously as the orders are placed by computer. This does not mean that you will get it at the price that you see on screen, but it should be fairly close.

Limit Order

As you may guess from the name, the limit order tells the broker that there is a limit to the price you want to buy or sell at.

So if you are buying with a limit order you state the maximum that you want to pay, and this is usually just below the current market price. If and when the price goes that low, then the broker will "fill" or complete the order, provided the price stays down long enough.

What this means is that you are guaranteed you will not pay more than your limit price for the trade, and you could possibly but not usually pay slightly less. However, because of this you may find that the trade never takes place if the price does not drop sufficiently.

Take care that you do not place a limit order and forget it when it is not filled immediately. Make sure you keep a list of your open orders, and cancel any that you no longer require.

The sell limit order is similar to the buy limit, but in this case the price is set slightly higher than the current level. In effect, it is the least amount that you will accept. Once again, this means that the order may never be fulfilled, but guarantees you will get the price you ask for if possible.

Stop Order

There are various ways to use the stop order. One which you will use a lot is the stop loss order, which is often placed at the same time as your original order. If your trade goes in the wrong direction, the stop loss order is your safeguard to close the trade before it loses you too much.

So if you are going "long", looking for an increase in price, your stop loss order would be placed at a price less than you opened at. If the price dropped instead of going up, then your stop loss order could come into play.

Note that when your stop loss order price is reached, it becomes a market order to your broker to close your trade. It is usually not a problem, but this means that your broker will close your trade at the price which is current, which may not be quite the same as the price you set for the stop loss order.

Another use of the stop order is to open a position in the market. It may sound strange, but you could use a buy stop order set above the current price to open a long trade.

Why would you pay more than the current price? It depends on your strategy, but for instance you may have a feeling that the price will "break out" if it goes clear above a certain resistance level. If the price does not go above the resistance level, then there is no trade. If it does, you expect it to go higher and the trade is initiated by the buy stop order. Note that once again you have no guarantee of the price that the order happens at; it is just the market price when the trade happens.

Trailing Stop Order

Many brokers offer this frequently used order. It is a "moving" stop order. It can be used for both long and short trades, and as an example consider a long trade.

Your stop loss order would typically be below your opening price, and at a set value. A trailing stop order may be at a similar value below the opening price when you start, but as and when the price goes up, the value applied to the trailing stop goes up too, following a set distance behind the market price.

The key to the trailing stop order is that it is "on a ratchet", that is it never goes back down even if the price comes down. If the price keeps going up, the trailing stop keeps following behind. If the price starts back down, the trailing stop stands its ground and if the price drops enough the trade is closed automatically, in a similar way to the stoploss order. This has the effect of locking in much of the increase in value.

Discipline

Of course you know you will stick with your strategies, and keep trading well. Right now, there is no reason to think anything else.

When you are in the heat of battle, second-guessing your last move, figuring out the amount you lost last time in your head, and wondering whether you really have a good trading plan, you will find it very hard to maintain your discipline and keep a cool head.

You will be tempted to learn short-term lessons from the way the market has treated you, and react instinctively rather than in a planned manner. The trouble is that your normal instincts are not suited to this environment, and can even be destructive to your account.

Believe me, I know you are claiming otherwise, but you will be surprised at yourself when real money is on the line.

Confidence

One way to counter this urge is to have true confidence in your trading plan. Your trading plan should be fully prepared before you ever risk any money, and you need to know in your heart that it can succeed. This is one reason that it is very difficult to buy a trading plan from an "expert" and put it to work.

I'm not saying that investing in premade trading plans is doomed, just that it is more difficult than simply paying your money and expecting a magic button. You always need to be learning, and one way to learn is to observe how others trade. But having done that, you should then take the parts that suit you and your style of trading, and prove them thoroughly for your circumstances.

Patience

Part of discipline is having the patience to wait for the right trades to turn up. It can seem that you are not "working at it" if you don't have active positions open, and the urge to open a half right trade can be strong. However you must wait for trades that are fully in keeping with your plan, otherwise you risk scuppering your strategy.

Control

It is interesting to consider how much control you are able to exercise in your trading. You have the most control just before you enter a position, when you have time to review your various indicators and chart values, and decide whether conditions are right.

Once you have entered a trade, the situation changes completely and there are many possibilities to which you must react appropriately. The market does not care that you exist or that you have decided which way it "should" go.

Oddly enough, you have most control in this situation when you are losing. You simply have to have the discipline to cut your losses either when your stoploss position is reached, or earlier if there are reasons to believe that your initial premise was wrong.

On the other hand, if you're winning you have very little control, and no way to affect whether it is a big win or a small one. All you can control is when you exit the trade, and while you don't want to do this too early and lose possible profit, you are responsible for exiting and protecting any profits made, perhaps through a trailing stop loss order.

Psychology

I cannot over emphasize the importance of your psychology to whether you win or lose. You must have the mental ability to accept losses and profits as they are dealt to you, and not allow your emotions to be unreasonably aroused.

You may be surprised how difficult it is to behave rationally when real money is at stake, when you may see it slipping away from you. No amount of practice or study can equip you for the emotions you will feel, and mastering the psychology of trading is one of the hardest but most necessary tasks facing you if you are to become a successful trader.

Removing emotions from trading is a difficult task, but you can help yourself by having a clear trading plan which guides your decision-making. Having a plan, even a potentially winning one, is only a first step unless you can manage to implement it through thick and thin.

One of the tools to help you is a trading journal, where you write down each of your trades and the reasons that you placed it. You should also note how you feel emotionally at the time. This will allow you to monitor your performance and learn from your mistakes.

You should take care not to beat yourself up too much if you deviate from your trading plan at first. Sometimes you will, and sometimes it will work out better, which made tempt you to deviate more in future. Be aware that no one is born with a native instinct for trading, and the more you can stick with your plan the better your results should be. Occasionally you will want to review your trading plan to see if you can improve the results, but this should be a measured review and not just a reaction to a bad trading day.

Planning

Now we come down to some strategies and tactics. The first point to make is that you do not need to make things more complicated than necessary. Often complexity will just make your trading plan more difficult or time-consuming to follow with only the possibility of marginal gains.

Winning traders often only use simple approaches, but they use them consistently. Even a poor plan with good money management is going to outperform a good plan poorly implemented. Your focus must be on trading consistently and steadily.

You must create a trading plan that you can follow whatever the market does. It has to be complete, with actions to be taken for any circumstances. Only then can you properly gauge your performance, and have a consistent history to look over to see where you can improve.

Every trading plan includes an entry, where you are in complete control, and an exit, on which you have a variable amount of control. If you are in a losing position, then your exit is compelled once you reach a certain point; when you're winning, you have the choice of settling for a certain amount of profit if you think that is all you can get, or waiting to see if it gets better still; you also may choose to exit a trade which goes nowhere at all, to free up your capital for another trade.

Types of Market

There are basically three types of market or price action. It is important that you identify what particular phase the market you are interested in is going through, as each will require a different approach. In fact, you may decide to only trade when a certain pattern is being followed.

Trending

You can choose to find a currency pair which is exhibiting a strong trend, and trade with the trend taking a long or short position that assumes the trend will continue. You would look for indicators that suggest a strong and continuing price movement, and consider exiting the trade on a trailing stop loss or when you could see weakness in your indicators.

Breakouts

Another technique is to look for conditions that will give a sharp move in price, or a breakout from the current range of movement. This often happens with a reversal, but may also be seen when a price has been going sideways, or trading in a range, and then makes a shift outside the range.

Range Trading

An alternative is to find prices that are trading in a range, and simply trade frequently to capture small gains from the oscillations in price. In this case the possible profit is clearly defined and limited for each trade, and usually the spread between buying and selling prices becomes more significant because of the small amount of price movement that you are seeking to capture. Nonetheless, this can be a consistent way to grow your profits.

Making an Entry

Just like the serve in tennis, this is the one place where you have absolute authority, and can start however you want. But it is a mistake to think that you can, with enough effort, develop a perfect entry signal. When you choose your entry conditions, all you're doing is improving your chances of making a winning trade.

The exact parameters that you choose to use to "trigger" your trade will depend on the type of market that you are trading. We will look at some examples later, but basically they may be based on patterns, moving averages, or other indicators.

None of these is infallible, and they can all produce false signals, in the sense that the market goes a different way from what you expect.

And it is not the case that the more indicators you use, the more "accurate" or profitable you can expect your entry to be. In fact, if you try and use too many indicators you may finish up with "analysis paralysis", unable to make a confident decision.

Possibly the best way to work out which indicators you want to use is to bring up several charts typical of the trading that you will be doing, and bring up each indicator in turn. By looking at where each indicator would signal an entry you can see which ones work well and which would mislead you for the type of trading you're doing.

Once again, you must bear in mind that there is no perfect entry signal and that every indicator will give you false signals at times.

You're just looking for the indicators that work most often.

Your trading plan should include more than one trade indication. This says that regardless of the trading signal you decide on, you will require the chart to satisfy another condition before initiating the trade. For instance, if your entry signal is proposed to be a moving average crossover, even when the moving averages cross you may not take the trade until a particular oscillator is moving in the right direction, and above a certain value.

One way to think of this is that you have "triggers" and "conditions". The condition must be right, whether it is an indicator or simply the price above a certain moving average, before you act on the triggering event, such as a crossover.

Particularly in the case where you are looking for breakouts or reversals, you could incorporate the need for "confirmation" before trading. This is simply waiting after you get the signal to make sure that the price is really going in the right direction. While you can lose a little profit by delaying your trade, it might be worthwhile if, say, 20% of the time the signal does not work and the price goes in the wrong direction.

Exit Considerations

The prime rule is to cut your losses and let your winners run. In many ways the exit decision is more important than the entry. It is only when you close your trade that you determine whether or not you have made any money, and if so how much.

This leads to a discussion of the three types of exit decision you will face.

Losing Exits

One of the most difficult things you will face is closing a losing trade in a timely way. But it is what separates those who make a good job of trading and the "also-rans".

It is easy to see why it is a problem. When you close your trade to cut your losses you must accept that the trade did not work, in other words you feel that your decision to buy was wrong and you made a mistake. This is an uncomfortable feeling, and one that most people try and avoid. The thought is that while you're hanging onto your trade it could always turn around and prove you right, but if you close it you have to face the facts.

You have to counter this by having a plan for when you will sell at a loss, and sticking to it. After all, it is no big thing. No one on this earth knows which direction the market will go tomorrow, and if it goes in the opposite direction to your trade it does not prove you are "wrong". If you have traded according to your trading plan, and that plan has been compiled with care and thought, then even your losing trade is a "right" trade.

One way to make this losing exit a little easier is to use the stoploss order. Some people warn against putting your "stops" in the market, as they feel that unscrupulous dealers if they are market makers and have a dealing desk can manipulate the prices, perhaps taking you out of the trade before moving the prices in the other direction. If you share this view, you should at least have a written note of where you will close the trade so that you cannot cheat when under emotional pressure.

Given that you accept the need to fix and stick with a stoploss, there are various ways that you can come up with the value or price that you will allow the trade to go to before exiting.

Technical Stop

From your technical analysis, you may have determined a level at which you know that your trade has failed. For instance, if your analysis includes support and resistance levels, perhaps the breach of one of these would confirm that your trade is a loser. You can position your stop loss just outside this value, allowing a little slack for the inevitable approximations.

Percentage Stop

Another simple method is to calculate your stoploss based on losing a certain percentage of the price. If you do this, be sure to review the chart to see the amount of volatility that can be expected, as otherwise you might find that this stop loss is triggered not for a losing position but simply because of natural fluctuations.

A similar method is to calculate your stoploss based on a fixed change in price.

Volatility Stop

To counter the chance of being "stopped out" of an otherwise profitable position, you can incorporate volatility into your calculation. The Average True Range (ATR) is an indicator that gives you the volatility over the previous number of days. Frequently, traders will allow the price to vary by twice the ATR before it hits the stoploss.

This is an example of the ATR on MetaTrader 4. The lower window shows the values which as you can see are forever changing. For this range of chart, they vary between 0.0056 and 0.0095 – this is a 4 hourly EURUSD chart.

If you had say gone long on the moving average crossover just to the right of center, the corresponding value would have been just over 0.007, so your stop loss could be set at 0.014 below your entry price. With an entry price of about 1.336, your stop loss level would be 1.336 minus 0.014, or 1.322. This is actually about the level of the previous low point, the bottom of the white candle. If you had been using a technical stop level, that might have been the level you chose anyway, so this provides confirmation. You can see it easier on this blow up picture: -

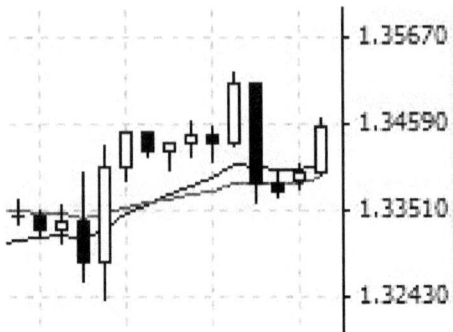

Obviously, this trade worked out well, with a retracement to just above 1.3351 before the uptrend continued, and the stop loss would not have been activated.

Winning Exits

"Let your winners run" is the best advice here, but you need to understand how to do that. Typically, you may use some kind of trailing exit which will follow up behind the price, but not go back down again so that as and when the price reverses, the trade is closed near the top.

This was mentioned previously as a "trailing stop", which many brokers will offer, or you can do it manually by keeping a track of the price. The key to the trailing stop is the idea of a ratchet on the price, so that it can go up (for a long trade) as the price rises, but never down. The same idea applies to the short trade.

Of course, some people say you "never go broke taking a profit". They are wrong. Taking profits too early is the reason that many traders fail, as you need to realize the potential gains to offset the inevitable losses. It's easy, particularly after a few losses, to want to close the trade quickly and secure the profit, giving yourself a good feeling in the process.

On the other hand, no one can pick the peak in a price until after it has happened. So a trailing exit is one way to secure most of the profit, even though it inevitably leads a little margin behind.

Thinking about the stoploss, you can apply similar calculations to the way you set up your trailing exit. For the most part, these are nuances and not terribly significant. The main point is that you do have a trailing stop to lock in your profits.

Technical Trailing Stop

To have a technical trailing stop you must analyze the chart and decide at what stage the price has run out of steam, and is looking as though it could reverse, as opposed to undergoing a small retracement in a solid trend.

For the example above, as mentioned the initial stoploss level could have been set at the previous low, at 1.324. For a technical trailing stop, you could shift this stoploss order up to 1.335, the next low, and then 1.357 after it passes this point on the main chart.

In each case, the higher low after a retracement shows that the trend is continuing – it is the definition of the trend. So if the price comes back down below you are happy to close the trade, knowing that the trend is failing.

Percentage Retracement

The trailing stop could be set to follow the price at a certain percentage distance, and this is a common sort of order that would be available to you. You have to use common sense in deciding on the percentage, bearing in mind the volatility that you are seeing, simply so that you do not set the numbers so close to the price that your trade gets stopped out on normal fluctuations.

Another use of the percentage is to set the stop at a certain percentage of your potential profit. For instance, you might think that you should set it 20% away from the price. At first, it will be very close to the price, but later it will give the price more room for fluctuations. The percentage you choose will depend on your trading timeframe, as well as the strength of the trend.

Volatility Trailing Stop

Similar to the stoploss order, you could set a trailing stop to be a multiple of the ATR from the price. This allows the volatility to change, but still accommodates what may be expected to be normal fluctuations without causing the trade to be closed.

Once again this is used as a trailing stop, and the level must never be allowed to go back, but only ratcheted up as necessary.

"Time Out" Exits

This type of exit is often overlooked in trading plans and in literature. In some trades, the volatility dries up and the price goes nowhere. Even if you are not showing a loss, you are not gaining from sitting in the trade and waiting when you could be doing something else that is hopefully more profitable with your money and time.

It is a personal matter for you how long you are prepared to wait before you see any action, and how patient you can be. Just be aware that there are other things you could be doing rather than sitting and watching a price which flat lines its way across the chart. If you lose a little on the spread it could be worth it in order to get your money working again.

Sample Strategy

Note that this section is included to show you how you can put together a trading plan. I make no representations whatsoever about the ideas put forward, and whether you would profit or lose by using them. It is up to you to put together your own trading plan, using values and indicators you select, and to test it to your own satisfaction.

I recommend that you "back test" your system, if you have a facility so to do. Frequently charting programs allow you to run back tests on historic data, seeing how your plan would have performed over the years. Past performance is no guarantee of future results, but if you find values of variables and indicators that would have worked in the past, you may choose to use these going forward in the hope that they will continue to work.

As we have looked at the moving average and RSI in previous sections, I will explain how these can be combined into a trading plan.

Looking first for potential long trade conditions, we will say that the market is bullish and supportive of an uptrend if the price is above a medium-term moving average line, say the SMA (60), and the RSI is above the center or 50% line. These are the "conditions" that we are looking for before we are able to place a long trade. Now all we have to do is define the trigger.

For a trigger, we could consider that if the price has come down to the trendline and started returning, continuation of the uptrend is indicated. Similarly, if the price has come down below the trendline but returned, a "bearish failure", this is a strong indication that the bulls still rule the market and the price will go up.

Here's a likely candidate on the 4 hour EURUSD: -

The SMA (60) is going up and below the price, and the RSI (14) is above the halfway 50% level. I have shown a trendline connecting two low points on this uptrend, and the price is coming down to test whether this will hold. At this stage, the potential trade would be on your watch list – there is no trade for our plan yet, but if the price finds support on the trendline and starts back up, that is the time to move.

Moving on: -

After three more candles, 12 hours on this chart, the trade is coming up. The price has touched the trendline, and the next candle trades clear above the line, providing an indication that the support has held.

The next period opens at 1.42880, so you can place a trade as the price is still going up. Your stop loss could be situated at the trendline level, say 1.42567, giving a potential loss of 31 pips if the trade fails. The previous peak was 143 pips above the trendline, so the risk-reward ratio is good.

Here is the continuation: -

You can see that this time it worked out well, with a climb to as high as 1.44860 on the next surge. How much you make depends on your exit strategy, which could be a trailing stop at twice the ATR (about 80 pips) behind, therefore closing the position at about 1.4406 for a gain of 118 pips.

Incidentally, you can see that the same setup occurred again, with the price coming down to the trendline and going back up. In this case, the price faltered a little but may still have worked out as a gain.

This is one of many ways that you can combine your knowledge of the charts to potentially spot winning trades. You are not restricted to the indicators explained in this book, as most of them work on the same principle of indicating overbought and oversold conditions, and you can experiment by putting them on the charts you are looking at.

Even when have you have decided on your indicators, you can do further research into the parameters that you use. Be careful to do just enough research, and not get stuck with "analysis paralysis", as you will never perfect your trading plan. Take what you find to be a workable system, and practice with it on a demo or free account until you have confidence that it will on balance give you a profit.

Appendix – Forex Robots

If you're anything like me, you have probably been sucked in by the lure of one or more of the descriptions of black box trading robots. They employ effective copywriters who pull the right strings to part you from your money.

They will even tackle the question of why they are choosing to make money selling their Forex robot, or software program, rather than just using it and making a fortune. Something on the lines of the pious "wanting to give something back", or "the market is large enough that no matter how many people use it, it will not affect my personal profits".

It is so hard to think that the robot will not make some positive difference. The advertising copy for F... T... claims that the robot is capable of "Doubling Your Money Every Single Month". It only costs $149 – what a bargain!

But wait. If this software can really double your money every month, then starting with $1000 you could make over $8 billion in just two years. Why sell it to others? The stock answer that they "invest the profits from sales into the trading accounts" just does not seem to hold water – in other words the sales profits should be a drop in the ocean compared to the trading gains in accordance with their claims.

The point is that robots will work some of the time, and I personally have tested them. I got quite excited when one steadily grew a demonstration account by 10% in one month, only to find that it gave back all those profits in one loss a few days later. Much of the time they can get away with it by having a distant stoploss which allows the market to swing back and forth until the target profit is reached – but if the price goes all the way to the stoploss, then you lose a lot at once.

If you study the markets and take on technical analysis, then you are able to perform better than any software. You have a natural ability to be able to step back and look at the whole situation, rather than plowing on with a preprogrammed routine. Certainly a trading plan sounds very similar to a software program, but you are able to look at the big picture. The Forex robot gives a specific answer to a specific question, as programmed, and with few if any exceptions is not capable of dealing with "maybes".

Above all, do you really want to put your trading capital in the hands of a computer program that you don't have access to and wouldn't understand if you did? Who do you complain to when it blows out your account?

About the Author

Alan Northcott has been writing and educating in the financial sector for many years and now resides in Florida. His books have been featured on www.better-trades.com, and attract comments from venerable traders such as Greg Morris.

In addition to works published in his own name, Northcott has been responsible for the production of several trading courses, e-books and countless articles.

Other Books

In this series –

Options Trading – A Newbies' Guide

"Alan's Newbies Guide breaks down options trading to the newbie level in an easy to understand and follow style." – Usiere

Other titles by Northcott –

The Complete Guide to Investing in Short Term Trading

The Complete Guide to Using Candlestick Charting

The Complete Guide to Investing in Gold and Precious Metals

The Mutual Funds Book

The Hedge Funds Book

Asset Protection for Business Owners and High Income Earners

The Complete Guide to Investing in Derivatives

For full reviews, see book listings on www.amazon.com.